The Library of
NATIVE AMERICANS

The Caddo

of Texas

Lucile Davis

The Rosen Publishing Group's
PowerKids Press™
New York

To my mom, Rosemary Davis, my faithful proofreader

The editors wish to thank Robert Cast, Tribal Historic Preservation Officer for the Caddo Nation of Oklahoma, for his expertise.

Published in 2003 by The Rosen Publishing Group, Inc.
29 East 21st Street, New York, NY 10010

Photo and Illustration Credits: Cover and pp. 16, 20, 34, 37, 50 courtesy Cultural Preservation Department, Caddo Nation of Oklahoma (p. 50 by Silvermoon II); p. 4 Erica Clendening; p. 6 © D. Robert & Lorri Franz/CORBIS; p. 11 © David Muench/CORBIS; p. 13, 46, 49 © CORBIS; p. 14 © Lake County Museum/CORBIS; p. 19, 38, 42 © Bettmann/CORBIS; p. 22 Trustrim Connell Collection RC 5(1):34, Heard Museum, Phoenix, Arizona; p. 25 © Buddy Mays/CORBIS; p. 26 © Craig Aurness/CORBIS; p. 28 © Bohemian Nomad Picturemakers/CORBIS; p. 31 © G.E. Kidder Smith/CORBIS; p. 33 courtesy Canyon Records (6146); p. 45 © Gerald French/CORBIS; p. 49 Library of Congress Geography and Map Division, Washington, D.C.; p. 53 © Danny Lehman/CORBIS.

Book Design: Erica Clendening

Davis, Lucile.
      The Caddo of Texas / Lucile Davis.
            p. cm. — (The library of Native Americans)
      Summary: Describes the history, culture, government, beliefs, and current situation of the Caddo.
      Includes bibliographical references and index.
      ISBN 0-8239-6435-3
      1. Caddo Indians—Texas—Juvenile literature [1. Caddo Indians. 2. Indians of North America.]
I. Title. II. Series.
E99.C12 D44 2002
976.4004'979—dc21

                                        2002004093

There are a variety of terminologies that have been employed when writing about Native Americans. There are sometimes differences between the original language used by a Native American group for certain names or vocabulary and the anglicized or modernized versions of such names or terms. Although this book contains terms that we feel will be most recognizable to our readership, there may also exist synonymous or native words that are preferred by certain speakers.

Contents

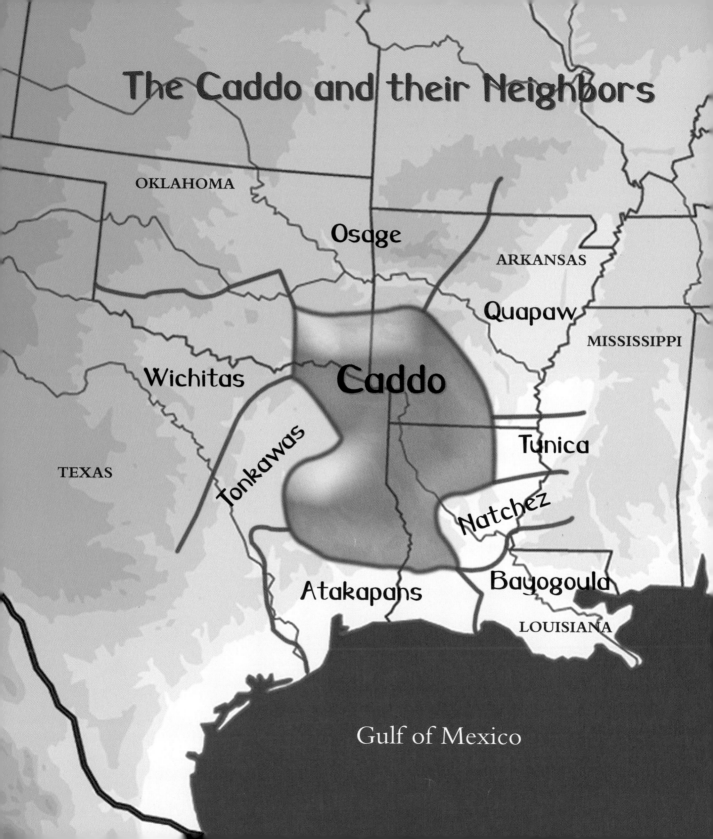

The Caddo and their Neighbors

OKLAHOMA

Osage

ARKANSAS

Quapaw

MISSISSIPPI

Wichitas

Caddo

TEXAS

Tonkawas

Tunica

Natchez

Atakapans

Bayogoula

LOUISIANA

Gulf of Mexico

One

An Introduction to the Caddo

The Caddo Native Americans named the state of Texas. In the Caddoan language, *tayshas*, or *taychas*, means "friends" or "allies." It is what the peoples of the Caddo confederacies, or unions of tribes, called each other. The Europeans began to call the Caddo by that name. Eventually Caddo territory became known as Tayshas, or "the Kingdom of the Tejas." The Spanish pronounced the word "Tejas" (teh-HAS). English speakers pronounced it "Texas."

The Caddo confederacies played an important role in the history of Texas. Among the Native American groups in the state, they were the most successful farmers. They also had a stable government and well-ordered society. The Caddo united many of the Native American groups living around them through a complex trade network. Some chiefs of the confederacies acted as representatives between rival governments.

The name Caddo is a contraction of Kadohadacho. The head of a Caddo tribe was called the *caddi*, which means "chief." *Hadacho*, by some translations, means "tough" or "unyielding." Roughly translated, Kadohadacho means "real chief" or "true chief."

There were three Caddo confederacies: Kadohadacho, Hasinai, and Natchitoches. The Kadohadacho was the strongest of the three confederacies. When the Caddo went to war to protect themselves or their

This map shows the areas where the Caddo lived, in present-day Texas, Oklahoma, Arkansas, and Louisiana.

territory, it was usually a Kadohadacho who led the warriors into battle. The Kadohadacho lived in the areas now known as northeast Texas, southwest Arkansas, and southeast Oklahoma. The Hasinai confederacy was the largest. These people lived along the upper Neches and Angelina River valleys in East Texas. The third confederacy, the Natchitoches, lived in present-day Louisiana.

A common language and way of life joined the people of the Caddo confederacies. They hunted deer, turkey, and other animals, and gathered roots, nuts, and wild fruit until they learned how to plant and harvest crops. This knowledge came from other Native American groups living in what are now the Southern states. These tribes were mound builders. Like some of the natives of South America, they built their villages around a mound used for religious ceremonies. The Caddo were mound

The Caddo hunted deer and other animals.

builders also. The mounds were flat-topped platforms of earth created as the building site of their religious leaders' home and temple. The mounds were also the burial site for the tribal leaders.

When the Europeans encountered the Caddo in 1541, the Caddo were settled, successful farmers. The area where the Caddo lived surrounded all the major rivers and drainages in present-day northeast Texas, southwest Arkansas, northwest Louisiana, and southeast Oklahoma.

The Spanish traveled up the Mississippi River from New Spain (present-day Mexico) around the middle of the 1500s to claim territory for their king. French explorers went down the big river in the late 1600s and claimed the area for their king. Both the French and the Spanish hoped to persuade the Caddo to help them with their land claims. The Caddo found themselves in the middle of their dispute. It was a position of power. The Caddo traded with the Europeans, but did not take sides.

When settlers from the United States began to move west, the Caddo again found themselves in the middle of another dispute. The United States wanted to settle the territory west of the Mississippi. The Spanish were determined to hold on to the lands now known as Texas, New Mexico, and parts of Colorado. Once again, the Caddo traded with both sides, but stayed out of the fight.

By the middle of the 1800s, the Caddo were no longer in a position of power. The United States moved them from their lush green forestland to dusty Oklahoma. The Caddo, however, did not disappear into the wind-driven dust of Oklahoma. They survived and moved on just as they had thousands of years earlier.

Creation Myth

Caddo grandfathers have told of a time when everything was dark. There was no sun, moon, stars, or earth. Time passed, and a man appeared. He was the first human. Soon a village sprang up. Thousands of people lived in the village. The people saw the first man. They did not know him, but he seemed to be everywhere.

The man disappeared for a time. When he returned, he brought all kinds of seeds with him. He gave them to the people. He said the seeds were for eating. Then he told them Darkness would go and leave the people a man by the name of Sah-cooh (Sun). Sah-cooh would be given much power by Ah-ah Ha'-yo, or the Great Father Above. The unknown man told the people the direction the Sun came from should be called "east." The direction the Sun went to should be called "west."

The unknown man said that when the time came he would be called to leave his Great Mother Earth Below to join the Great Father Above. Until then, he said he had work to do. Then he began to instruct the people. He told them they must have one wise and able man for their leader. The leader must be called the caddi. The people were to obey the caddi and look upon him as a great father. He told the people to select a caddi.

The people went away to select a caddi. They selected the unknown man and gave him a name. They called him Neesh, meaning "Moon." Neesh became the leader and selected a tamma, or an errand man. This man went around to all the people to tell them when Moon wanted them.

One day the tamma *called the people saying Neesh, the Moon, wanted them to come together quickly. When the people came together, Moon said it was time to go away from their dark world. Before they left, Moon told them to divide into groups. Each group must have a leader, Moon told them. These leaders should be called* canaha.

When the groups were formed and leaders chosen, Moon told the people to sing and beat the drums. They were to move forward and never look back. The first to climb up into the light was an old man. He carried fire and a pipe in one hand and a drum in the other. His wife followed him into the light carrying corn and pumpkinseeds. All the people and animals moved forward toward the light. One man, called Wolf, saw the light-filled world and told Moon it was too small to hold everyone. He turned to see how many people were behind him. Those who had not stepped into the light stopped and went back. The people in the light sat down and cried for those who were left in darkness. Where they sat down is known as Cha-cah-nee-nah, the "Place of Crying."

The people headed in the same direction as the Sun. As they traveled west, Moon picked up dirt and threw it in front of him, creating high mountains. The people stopped and began to build homes and villages. Moon went to the top of the mountain and saw that not all the people had followed him. When the people came up into the light, they all spoke one language—Caddo. Now they were scattered in different directions and spoke different languages.

Where the Caddo Came From

Some anthropologists believe the Caddo came from a large group of people living in the southeast portion of North America. A similarity in the Caddo and Iroquois languages has led some anthropologists to believe the two groups lived together at one time. These anthropologists believe that about 3800 B.C. the two groups began to separate. The Iroquois settled along the East Coast. The Caddo traveled west toward the Great Plains.

Some anthropologists believe the ancestors of the Caddo came from the Caribbean. The Caribbean area is located off the northeast coast of South America. It includes the Caribbean Sea and a small string of islands. A group of Caribbean people may have traveled by water to the Gulf Coast and settled somewhere in the area of what is now Florida, Georgia, and Alabama sometime before 500 A.D.

Whether the Caddo came from the Caribbean, or southeastern North America, they traveled west. Caddoan-speaking people settled as far west as the Rocky Mountains. But the main group of people who would become known as Caddo settled in the forests just west of the Mississippi River.

The date the Caddo people began living in this area is thought to be around 1200. However, the Caddo could have begun living in this area at least 7,500 years ago. There is evidence for this in the discovery of the Conly Site on Loggy Bayou near the Red River. This site has the oldest human remains ever discovered in the state of Louisiana. These remains will be returned to the Caddo Nation.

The Caddo were hunters and gatherers. They hunted game and gathered fruit, nuts, and roots for food. They were organized into small bands. These bands moved around as they followed the game animals.

The Caddo came to settle west of the Mississippi River.

About 500 B.C. they learned how to plant and harvest crops. This changed their way of life. Instead of traveling in small groups, they came together in larger groups to plant crops. They built permanent villages and developed an organized way of life around different levels of leaders.

The Caddo and Their Neighbors

Their success as farmers made the Caddo the dominant group in what is now the western parts of Arkansas and Louisiana, east Texas, and southeast Oklahoma. The Ais and the Adaes were Caddoan-speaking tribes living between the Hasinais in east Texas and the Natchitoches in Louisiana. The Ais and Adaes were not part of the Caddo confederacies. Trade with the Caddo helped keep these two tribes alive.

The Tonkawas lived west of the Hasinais. They were nomads who hunted the buffalo on the central Texas plains. The Tonkawas also traded with the Caddo. The Wichitas were among the strongest of the Caddo neighbors. Their language was similar to Caddoan. They planted crops and lived in villages. Unlike the Caddo, though, the Wichitas relied on the buffalo for their main food source, clothing, and tools. The Kichais were a tribe of people with a culture similar to the Wichitas. The Kichais were of Caddoan ancestry and lived north of the Tonkawas. Both the Wichitas and the Kichais maintained close ties with the Caddo confederacies.

The Caddo built a large trade network. It helped them guarantee the friendship of the Native American groups around them. Some groups, however, were not interested in trade or friendship. The Osage were one of those tribes. This Siouan tribe lived in what is now Missouri. The Osage and the Caddo were ancient enemies. The Osage raided Caddo territory. The Caddo struck back to take revenge. War between the Osage and Caddo did little damage to

This photo from the early 1900s shows Wichita children in their encampment.

either group—their wood, rock, and shell weapons could cause injury, but rarely caused death. That changed when the Europeans began to sell guns to the Native Americans. After the Osage and the Caddo acquired guns, their conflict became deadly.

The Apaches also were rivals of the Caddo. The Apaches arrived on the Great Plains in the fourteenth century. The Lipan Apaches settled on the Texas plains near the Caddo. The Lipan Apaches acquired horses and metal from the Spanish living in New Mexico.

This 1937 photo shows Apache Indians in their camp.

Their arrows and lances had metal points. Their raids on the Caddo were swift and deadly. Soon, the Caddo, also began to acquire Spanish horses and metal in trade from other tribes. The Caddo confederacies were able to put more warriors in the field. With horses and metal weapons, the Caddo were able to fight off the Apaches most of the time.

The Caddo fought with these tribes to protect their homes, families, and crops. The Caddo did not consider war a productive use of their time. Heroic deeds in battle could win a warrior status as an *amayxoya* (ah-may-sho-uh), or "war hero." However, the change in status did not bring the warrior wealth, or change his rank within Caddo society. For the Caddo, farming was more important than going to war.

Two

The Caddo Confederacies

From 500 B.C. until 1200 A.D. the Caddo settled into a farming way of life. Their territory lay between the Trinity and the Arkansas Rivers. During this time, they developed a well-structured social system and a strong religion.

By the end of the fifteenth century, the population of the Caddo culture had reached its high point. Some estimates say that over 200,000 Caddos lived in settlements. These settlements ranged from large, heavily-populated communities to small rural settlements. The Caddo cultural success was based on strong religious and social structure and the ability to cultivate a wide variety of crops, such as corn, pumpkins, sunflowers, squash, and beans.

Religion

At the head of each Caddo confederacy was a male religious leader. This leader was called *xinesi* or *chenesi*. Roughly translated, *xinesi* means "Mr. Moon." The *xinesi* was responsible for the religious life of the confederacy.

The Caddo religion centered on an all-powerful creator, known as Ah-ah Ha'-yo, or the Great Father Above. They believed this being watched over them and guided them. The creator guided

Homes of the Caddo religious leaders were built on temple mounds like these.

them through a pair of supernatural twin children. The twins were called *coninisi*, or "the little ones." The commands of the *coninisi* came from the Great Father Above and were passed on to the *xinesi*. That made the commands from the *xinesi* the word of the Great Father Above, and those words were strictly followed.

A *xinesi* served as religious leader for his entire life. This position in the confederacies was an inherited one. When a *xinesi* died, his closest male relative, such as a brother, son, uncle, or nephew, became the *xinesi*. In addition to bringing advice and commands from the *coninisi* to the Caddo people, *xinesi* performed religious ceremonies and watched over a sacred temple fire.

The Caddo people supplied the *xinesi* and his family whatever he needed. Food, clothing, and other items were brought to him by the *xinesi*. The *xinesi* lived in a large house built on the temple mound. A small house next to the temple was for the *coninisi*. When the old *xinesi* died, his house and temple were burned and covered with dirt. The people then built a new house and temple on top of the mound for the new *xinesi*. Other mounds were constructed as burial sites for the *xinesi* and other important people of the confederacies. These people were buried with many of their possessions.

Under the *xinesi* was a lesser class of priests. They were called *connas*. They used herb medicines and religious ceremonies to heal the sick. They also performed new house blessings and burial rites. There were medicine men guilds, or societies. These guilds held public initiations rites for new members. A celebration followed, with food, drink, and dancing. Initiates were given a drink brewed just for the occasion. The prospective medicine men drank until they fell down in a trance. The men would remain in a trance for 24 hours. When they awoke, they would tell of the dreams they experienced.

The Caddo played lacrosse for recreation.

The Caddo stopped building mounds sometime before they began to have contact with the Europeans. Even after contact with Europeans, the confederacies continued to look to the *xinesi* as their religious leaders. The temples and the *xinesi* lodges, however, were no longer built on mounds. Important people were no longer buried in mounds. They, and the rest of the villagers, were buried in large cemeteries. The custom of burying an individual with his possessions continued. The Caddo believed the individual would need his or her possessions while he or she remained in the place of waiting.

The Caddo were buried with their possessions, like this pottery vessel.

The Caddo believed when they died, they went to a place of waiting. They would stay there until all the Caddo were dead. Afterward, all the Caddo would go together to a beautiful land where everyone would live in happiness and harmony.

The Caddo believed all things in the natural world had a spirit. Human beings had no power over other creatures. All creatures of nature were equal. Before hunting, Caddo men asked their animal neighbors for the favor of a good hunt. The women thanked the plants for providing the Caddo with food. Caddos believed individuals could gain power through a supernatural helper.

The most important Caddo religious celebration was the ceremony of the first fruits. This ceremony celebrated the harvest.

Tribal Organization

Though the *xinesi* was a religious leader, he also acted as governor over his confederacy. Tribal leaders answered to him. A tribal leader was considered the most able, strongest man in the tribe. Other men served under him. A Caddo tribe's leader was called a *caddi*. The position of *caddi* was also an inherited one. The *caddi* stood as the decision maker for the tribe. He headed war expeditions, sponsored important tribal ceremonies, and conducted the peace pipe ceremony. When the *caddi* died, his closest male relative inherited the position.

22 This 1872 photo shows several Caddos sitting in front of a house.

Under the *caddi* was a *canahas*, who was a headman or village elder. He stood as head of the tribe if the *caddi* was away. There were also *chayas*, who took orders from the *canahas*.

The *tammas* were tribal messengers and policemen. On orders from the *caddi*, the *tammas* called the tribe together and made sure the gathering was orderly. They also carried out punishments issued by the *caddi*. The *tammas* were particularly watchful for those who might be slow or neglect to show up during planting season. A whipping was the usual punishment for this offense.

The Caddo worked together for the good of their communities. The people of a tribe worked together to plant crops and build homes. Tasks were divided between the men and the women. The men hunted, and the women made food, clothing, tools, and other useful articles from the dead animals. The men plowed and prepared the fields. The women sowed the seeds, weeded, watered, and then harvested the crop. Men built the lodges. Women made the furnishings for the lodge. The men made their own bows and arrows, garden hoes, moccasins, and other equipment. The women made everything else. At the age of about six or seven, children began to help out their parents.

Marriage and Childbirth

A young man courted a young woman by presenting gifts to her father. If the father allowed the young woman to accept the gifts, a marriage was contracted. The new couple moved in with the young woman's family.

Caddo marriages were not always permanent. If couples divorced, they did so without disgrace. Confederacy and tribal leaders were required to stay married.

When a couple divorced, the children stayed with their mother and her family. A boy's most important relatives were his mother's aunts and uncles. Male relatives would train him to be a warrior. Girls learned the homemaking arts and plant cultivation from their mothers, grandmothers, and aunts.

Childbirth had a specific ritual. When a woman approached the time to give birth, she left her home and built a small shelter close to a lake or stream. A forked tree limb or "clinging pole" was sunk into the ground in the middle of the shelter. As her labor pains began, the woman would crawl into her shelter and grasp the tree limb for support during the birth. Afterward, the mother immediately took her child to the river and bathed the baby. She carried her child back to her lodge and went on with her daily life. A week after the birth, a *connas* came to name the child. The naming ceremony included another bathing of the child, followed by a feast.

Caddo mounds can still be found today. This mound is in Toltec State Park, near Little Rock, Arkansas.

Three

Agriculture, Art, and Crafts

The Caddoan people lived in forest areas. There were no large fields for planting crops. Small areas of brush, grass, and fallen trees had to be cleared. This required a large workforce. All members of the Caddo tribes helped to clear the land and plant the crops. Men, women, and children worked the fields. Each plot of land was planted in order of rank, beginning with that of the *caddi.*

Caddos were good farmers. Corn was the Caddos' most important crop. They depended on it as the main food in their diet. For this reason, great care was taken in the planting, harvesting, and preserving of this staple. They used crop rotation and fertilizer to keep their fields productive. Crop rotation allowed the soil to rest. A field planted with corn one season would be planted with squash or pumpkins the next. The roots and vines of the squash or pumpkin plants helped hold the soil in place when it rained. Corn crops did not provide this kind of protection. The roots and vines of the squash and pumpkin plants also provided a new layer of fertilizer. The Caddo also used animal dung as fertilizer.

Caddos managed their crops well and kept two years' worth of seed for each crop they planted. The extra supply insured against disasters. If a crop was destroyed by bad weather, fire, or enemy raids, there would be enough seed left to replant the crop.

Corn was a staple crop of the Caddo.

The Caddo planted corn twice a year. The first crop was planted in April and harvested in May. This crop was known as "little corn" because the stalks and kernels of the corn were small. The second crop was planted in June. It grew tall and the ears produced large kernels. This corn was harvested in July. The fullest ears of corn were set aside for seed for the next planting. The corn harvested for food was stored in strong reed baskets and placed in small structures raised above the ground. Well-sifted

In order to keep the soil in a field healthy, crops were rotated: Corn would be planted one year, pumpkins the next.

ash was mixed with the corn to keep out worms. The baskets were tightly covered to keep out mice. The Caddo planted a variety of crops. They also raised pumpkins, watermelons, squash, beans, sunflowers, and tobacco.

Caddos farmed by hand. They did not make plows to hitch behind work animals. Their farm tools were simple, but effective. A hoe and a digging stick were their only tools. Hoes were made from the hipbones of deer or bear. Some hoes were made of fire-hardened walnut. Digging sticks were made of small tree limbs and were used to make holes for planting seeds.

Food and Cooking

The forests where the Caddo lived produced wild plants and fruit-bearing trees and bushes. Nut trees were plentiful. Women gathered leafy greens, herbs, and edible roots to add to the Caddo diet. Meals might include wild berries, cherries, or plums. Meat and fish were plentiful. The forest rivers were large enough for the Caddo to use multiple fishing lines to catch up to fifty fish at a time. Today, these multiple fishing lines are often referred to as "trout lines." Buffalo were hunted once a year, and the meat was dried into strips called jerky.

Between the Kadohadacho and the Hasinais lands was a place with a lot of sand. When this sand was boiled, it produced salt water. The salt water was used in cooking.

Shelter

The Caddo lived in communal shelters. Extended families of up to thirty people lived in these shelters or lodges. The lodges looked like haystacks or beehives and were made of grass bundles, logs, and poles. They stood about 50 feet (15.2 m) tall. The base of the lodge measured about 60 feet (18.3 m) in diameter.

A family that needed a new home notified the *caddi*. The tribal chief then set the construction date. He sent out the *tammas* to choose people to help build the house. On the assigned day, some men would bring large poles. Selected women would bring bundles of grass. Other people would dig holes in a circle pattern. A tall pole was placed in a hole in the center of the circle. This pole had a crossbar at the top. When all the circled holes were filled with poles, one man climbed to the top of the center pole. He drew the outer poles toward the center pole and tied them together. This was the lodge frame. Cross poles were tied to the lodge frame and the grass bundles were hung on the cross poles. When the lodge was finished, the family who would live there fed those who had built it.

The family furnished their lodge with floor mats, beds, shelves, baskets, and chairs. Floor mats were made of woven reeds. These reed mats were placed over pounded earth floors. The mats were often dyed various colors and painted with figures of animals and flowers. Beds were made of reed or cane mats laid on forked sticks.

Feather-stuffed deer skin or buffalo skins were placed over the mats. A buffalo skin or additional mats were hung at the sides of these beds to create a private sleeping place for each person.

These are modern replicas of Caddo homes in Anadarko, Oklahoma.

In the summer, open-sided shelters with roofs made of thatch—straw or reeds—were built for sleeping. Under the roof was a two-foot (.6 m) high platform for sleeping. The open sides of these shelters allowed the summer breezes to keep people cool as they slept.

Clothing and Body Decoration

In the summer, the men wore only breechcloths. A breechcloth is a piece of cloth or leather worn between the legs and held to the body by a string tied at the waist. The women wore calf-length leather skirts. Men and women wore moccasins, or went barefoot. Older children wore the same kind of clothes their parents wore.

In the winter, men wore leggings and bear robes to keep warm. Women wore poncho-like tops over their skirts and leggings under the skirts. The women also wore deerskin caps to keep warm.

After the Europeans came to North America, the Caddo began to wear European-style clothing made of cloth. Caddo men wore European-made shirts and coats with their breechcloths and leggings. The women wore shirts or ruffled blouses with their leather skirts.

Caddo men wore their hair two inches long. At the top of their heads, they allowed a section to grow longer. These sections were braided. The braids hung down to the men's waists. These braids could be decorated with metal pieces and feathers, or wrapped in fur. Most men shaved their heads, leaving a row of hair in the middle. The row of hair went from the forehead to the base of the skull. Bear grease was worked into the row of hair to make it stand up. Duck or swan down was stuck in this greased row of hair for special occasions.

This photo of modern-day Caddo shows them in traditional dress.

Men also wore jewelry, including necklaces, earrings, and nose rings. At first, jewelry was made from seeds, shells, and stones. As they began to trade for new materials, the Caddo made jewelry from glass beads, silver, and copper. When shiny metal became available to them, some men began to wear nose plates or pendants. The men pierced the area between the nostrils and hung a plate or pendant from it. Some pendants were large enough to cover a man's mouth. Some men wore plates big enough to hang down to their chins.

34   The Caddo were well known for their beautiful pottery vessels.

Caddo women wore their hair long. The custom was to part the hair in the center and pull it into a single braid at the back of the head. The braid was then worked into a knot secured at the nape of the neck. The hair could be decorated with metal pieces, bells, and feathers. Women also wore jewelry, including earrings, necklaces, finger rings, and bracelets.

Both men and women wore tattoos and body paint. Many Caddo, both men and women, wore a strip of tattooing from forehead to chin. Bands of tattoos were also worn around arms, wrists, ankles, and legs. Pictures of flowers, birds, and animals were worn on various parts of the body. Caddos created tattoos by pricking the skin until it bled. Charcoal was then worked into the wound. When it healed, the tattoo was permanent.

Arts and Crafts

Caddos created clothing art with paint and beadwork. Both men and women decorated their clothing and animal skins with pictures of flowers, animals, and mythical creatures. In early times, the Caddo used seeds, bones, and shells for beads. European goods came their way in trade during the sixteenth century. After that, the Caddo used European-made glass beads, metal decorations, and small bells on their clothing and moccasins.

Most clothing was made from tanned deerskin. Caddos were expert leather crafters and tanners. They used deer and buffalo brains to tan deerskins. Garments were fringed and decorated with beadwork.

Caddo women made pottery. These clay pieces were unique in both color and design. The women made bottle-like pottery with long necks. They also made bowls shaped like the keel of a ship. Some pottery designs were engraved with circle and scroll designs. Other designs were artistically created by using a variety of methods. Artists put their fingernail impressions into the clay, or stabbed the sharp point of a stick into the clay and dragged it across the vessel. They also added color to the vessels by rubbing red, white, green, and yellow pigments (including ochre, such as crushed hematite, limonite, or glauconite) on to the outside of the engraved vessels. These designs are unique to Caddo pottery.

The men crafted bows that were prized by all Native Americans who came within the Caddo trade circle. The bows were made from the wood of the Osage orange tree. The hard wood made the bow difficult to draw. An arrow shot from this bow, however, flew fast and true. It was said an arrow shot with this bow could go right through a buffalo.

Caddo pottery vessels, such as the one shown here, were often engraved with intricate designs.

Four

The Caddo and the Europeans

The Caddo first met the Europeans in 1541. The meeting was not friendly. The Spanish began to explore North America. Hernando de Soto had been sent to North America to establish colonies. He lost sight of that goal and began to search for gold. He and his army tramped through the southern region of the Mississippi River looking for rich Native American kingdoms. The Spanish tortured and killed many Native Americans in their search for gold. They also stole food and other supplies, then enslaved the Native Americans to carry what had been stolen from them. The Spanish army halted in present-day Arkansas to rest. A small force traveled south to explore. Perhaps the reputation for theft and murder preceded the Spanish, for the Caddo did not welcome them. The Spanish arrived on horses wearing full suits of armor. The small band of Spaniards was attacked. When the larger army came through, however, they passed without incident. They found a Caddo community. Again, the Caddo attacked. Both men and women fought the Spanish, and the Caddo triumphed. The Spanish soon left the area and returned to the Mississippi.

De Soto died the following year. His successor Luis de Moscoso decided to return de Soto's army to New Spain (present-day Mexico). De Moscoso headed west, straight into Caddo territory. The Spanish

This painting shows Hernando de Soto encountering the Mississippi River in 1541. At this time, he also encountered the Caddo.

Tonin's Prediction—A Caddo Legend

After the people came to the surface of the earth, Tonin joined them. Tonin was small, but he could do wonderful things. He could turn dark to light. If he wanted to travel, he only had to think of the place and he was there. When he wanted to hunt game all he had to do was point a finger and the animal fell dead. He could grant wishes. He could predict the future.

One day, he told the people he would leave them for six summers and six winters. He asked them to gather again in six days to watch him leave. The people gathered in six days. They watched as Tonin sang the song of death and rose into the sky. The people were sad, but they believed he would return.

After six years, many of the people forgot Tonin. One of Tonin's six brothers knew the time was near for Tonin's return. He gave the signal by beating his drum six times. Not everyone remembered the meaning of the signal.

That evening a bright star rose in the east. The people gathered to watch as Tonin descended. He talked with them half the night and told them of the future. He predicted a strange race of people would come into the land and frighten away the buffalo, deer, and bear.

Tonin stayed on Earth for awhile, but one day he called the people together. It was the last time. He said he would leave as before, but never return. He blessed the people, then rose in the sky.

raided a few Caddo villages. They stole the Caddo corn supply and took Caddos as slaves to carry it. Now and then, the Spaniards burned a village in an effort to force the Caddo to show them the way back to New Spain. The Caddo responded by leading the Spaniards in a circle. De Moscoso gave up and went back to the Mississippi. The Spanish built crude boats and floated down the big river to the Gulf of Mexico. Over a year later, what was left of de Moscoso's army finally reached the settlements of New Spain.

De Moscoso returned to Caddo country. Again, he and his army tramped through villages, stealing corn and taking slaves. On the return trip through these same villages, Spaniards found that the Caddo had recovered—their corn baskets were full again. No gold was found, however, so the Spanish left. The Caddo had no more contact with Europeans for 150 years.

The Caddo's first meeting with the French was friendlier. The Frenchmen's attitude may have made the difference. The Spanish were looking for wealth. The French were looking for a way home.

René-Robert Cavalier, Sieur de La Salle had explored the Mississippi from Canada to the Gulf of Mexico. He claimed the entire area for France and named it Louisiana. He went back up the Mississippi River and built Fort St. Louis in 1682. La Salle returned to France, seeking the financial support of the French king. He wanted to establish French colonies along the Mississippi. La Salle returned to North America and sailed into the Gulf of Mexico in 1684. He intended to travel up the Mississippi to Fort St. Louis, but

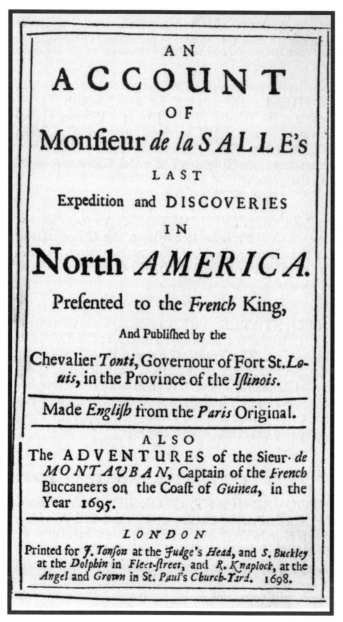

AN
ACCOUNT
OF
Monfieur *de la* SALLE's

LAST

Expedition and DISCOVERIES

IN

North AMERICA.

Prefented to the *French* King,

And Publifhed by the

Chevalier *Tonti*, Governour of Fort St. *Louis*, in the Province of the *Iflinois*.

Made *Englifh* from the *Paris* Original.

ALSO

The ADVENTURES of the Sieur· *de*
MONTAUBAN, Captain of the *French*
Buccaneers on the Coaft of *Guinea*, in the
Year 1695.

LONDON

Printed for *J. Tonfon* at the *Judge's Head*, and *S. Buckley*
at the *Dolphin* in *Fleet-ftreet*, and *R. Knaplock*, at the
Angel and *Grown* in St. *Paul's Church-Yard*. 1698.

missed the mouth of the river. He landed in what is now Texas. A series of mishaps followed and left La Salle without ships. He built a second Fort St. Louis in Texas. Leaving most of his people there, he took a group of twenty people and set off in search of the Mississippi. His plan was to make his way back up the big river to the established French colonies in Canada. There, he would find men and supplies to help him save the Texas colonists.

A Caddo man and his family found the Frenchmen trudging across the Texas prairie. The Frenchmen were in rags and starving. The Caddo man

42   This is the front page of La Salle's book describing his travels in North America. It was published in 1698.

invited the Frenchmen to his village. The French were received as honored guests. La Salle and his men stayed for a few days and traded their iron cooking kettles and axes for food and horses. The Caddo village impressed the Frenchmen. It was large, and the people seemed friendly and civilized. The lodges were well furnished. The beds and chairs in the lodges reminded the Frenchmen of their own homes. Life in the Caddo village seemed so good that when La Salle resumed his journey, four of the Frenchmen deserted and stayed with the Caddo.

The French experience at the Caddo village was a positive one. However, La Salle had noticed the Caddo possessed many Spanish goods. This made La Salle uneasy. The French and the Spanish were rivals for control of North America. La Salle determined he would return to the village to make allies out of the Caddo. In 1687, he began his return journey. For the next 100 years, both the French and the Spanish courted the Caddo with presents and trade.

The French settled in Louisiana Territory. The Spanish settled in New Spain and claimed all the land from what is now Mexico up into present-day Texas, New Mexico, and parts of Colorado. The Caddo lived in an area that lay across the claimed territories of both countries.

The Spanish courted the Caddo by establishing presidios, or forts, and missions in Texas. The Spanish believed they could "civilize" (make Christians of) the Caddo as they had the Pueblo Indians. The Spaniards had built walled missions protected by soldiers. The Pueblos had accepted the Spaniard's Catholic faith in order to live inside the mission walls, where they were safe from Apaches.

The Caddo did not need the Spaniards' protection, however. They had built their own protective wall. The Caddo believed the best defense was to surround themselves with trading partners. By the early 1600s, some estimates say there were about 200,000 Caddo. There were more than two dozen tribes living in the three Caddo confederacies. The Caddo people occupied the areas from present-day northeast Texas and Louisiana to the southern counties of Oklahoma. Their boundaries stretched from the Trinity River, in Texas, in the west, to the Ouachita River, in Arkansas and Louisiana, in the east. Gulf Coast tribes brought goods from Mexico for trade with the Caddo. Some tribes in what is now Kansas were also trading partners. The only flaw in the Caddo protection plan was the Osage Indians. Historic enemies of the Caddo, the Osage stole from them instead of making peace and trading.

The Spanish built missions, or religious communities, in Caddo territory, hoping to convert them to Catholicism. The Caddo came to the missions to trade for Spanish goods, but few stayed to become Catholics. The French took a different approach to their relationship with the Caddo. They set up trade with the Caddo. They were willing to trade guns for Caddo leather and salt. The Caddo were happy to get the guns. The guns helped them fight their old enemies, the Osage. The Spanish were unwilling to sell guns to Native Americans.

This is a picture of the Alamo. The part of the structure shown here was originally the front of the Mission San Antonio de Valero. It was fortified and used by Spanish and Mexican troops and U.S. defenders during fights between Texas and Mexico in the 1830s. It is remembered as the site of the last stand of Texan defenders of San Antonio in 1836.

45

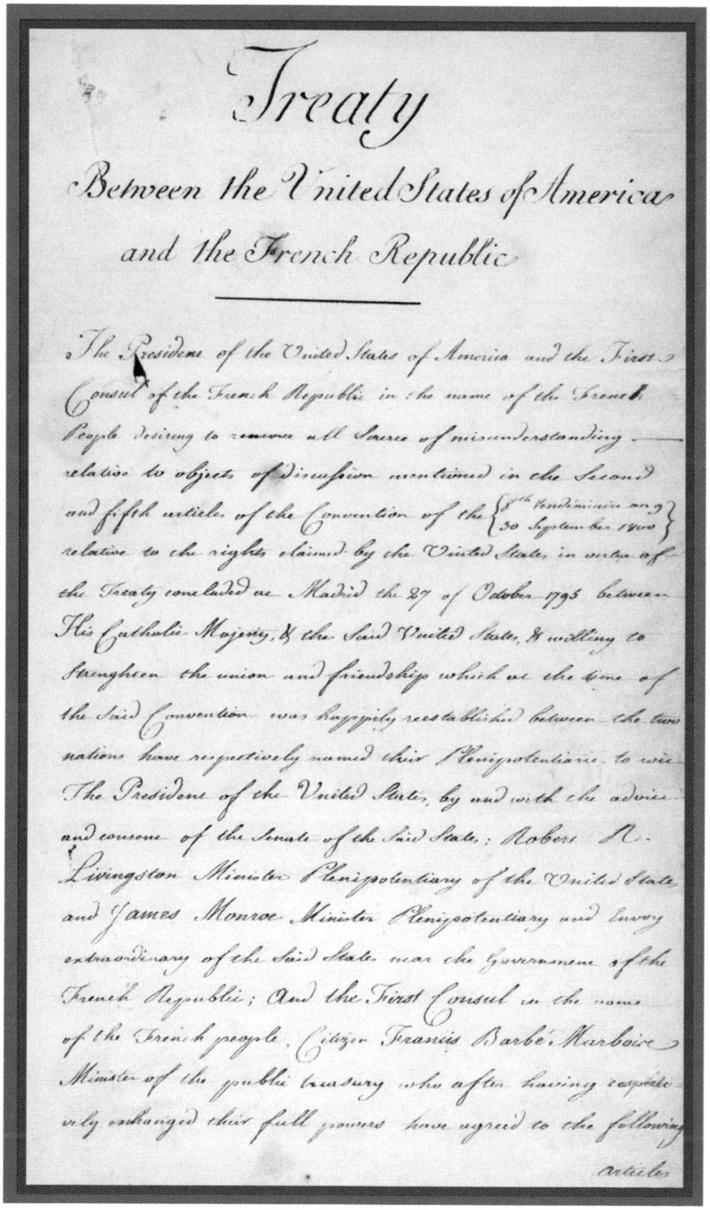

Treaty

Between the United States of America and the French Republic

The President of the United States of America and the First Consul of the French Republic in the name of the French People desiring to remove all Source of misunderstanding relative to objects of discussion mentioned in the Second and fifth articles of the Convention of the {8th Vendémiaire an 9 / 30 September 1800} relative to the rights claimed by the United States in virtue of the Treaty concluded at Madrid the 27 of October 1795 between His Catholic Majesty & the Said United States, & willing to Strengthen the union and friendship which at the time of the Said Convention was happily reestablished between the two nations have respectively named their Plenipotentiaries to wit The President of the United States, by and with the advice and consent of the Senate of the Said States; Robert R. Livingston Minister Plenipotentiary of the United States and James Monroe Minister Plenipotentiary and Envoy extraordinary of the Said States near the Government of the French Republic; And the First Consul in the name of the French people, Citizen Francis Barbé Marbois Minister of the public treasury who after having respectively exchanged their full powers have agreed to the following articles

In a secret treaty signed in 1762, the French turned the Louisiana Territory over to Spain, its ally in the French and Indian War, or the Seven Years' War, against England. The competition for Caddos as allies ended. Hard times fell on the Caddo confederacies. Contact with the Europeans had brought diseases to the Caddo. Epidemics of smallpox and other infectious diseases had reduced the Caddo population to around 20,000. The Osage took advantage of the situation. Armed with guns, the Osage began raiding further into Caddo territory.

In 1803, France sold the Louisiana Territory to the United States. This sale was called the Louisiana Purchase. The first page of the treaty is pictured above.

The Caddo still had a large trading network. They were also still considered the strongest Native American group in the area. There was, however, a new threat to the Caddo. Lipan Apache raids were carried out through Arkansas, Oklahoma, and down into Texas. The Apaches made no distinction between Native Americans and white settlers. They stole anything, particularly horses, from everyone and killed those who got in their way.

The Napoleonic Wars in Europe forced Spain to return the Louisiana Territory to France in 1800. In 1803, France sold it to the United States in what is known as the Louisiana Purchase. Once again, the Caddo found themselves caught between empires. The United States took over Louisiana. Spain still held the Texas territory. There was, however, an argument about boundary lines.

The exact boundary of the Louisiana Purchase had not been marked. Both the United States and Spain claimed the stretch of land between the two territories. The Caddo thought that land was theirs. During this time, a Caddo chief named Dehahuit played a major role in the conflict between the United States and Spain. Dehahuit acted as a representative between the two countries. He also kept peace among all the Native American nations in the area.

Dehahuit died in 1833 before the matter was resolved. By that time, however, the players had changed. In 1821, the Texas territory had become a part of the new Republic of Mexico. Three years after Dehahuit died, Texas declared itself independent of Mexico.

The boundary between the state of Louisiana and the Republic of Texas was resolved. The Caddo then found themselves being pushed off their land.

Settlers from the United States poured into Texas. Caddo land began to disappear behind fences, farms, and frontier towns. Bad weather, bad crops, and disease had reduced the Caddo population to around 2,000. Their trade network was gone. The animals they hunted for food and trade goods were almost gone. In 1845, when Texas became the twenty-eighth state in the United States, the Caddo were no longer needed as a buffer between arguing empires. Now, the Caddo were only in the way.

This is a map of the Province of Texas, drawn on cloth and labeled in Spanish. The map was drawn by Stephen Austin, the "Father of Texas," in 1822. When Texas became part of the United States in 1845, it marked a period of change for the Caddo.

49

Five

Caddo Survival

Raids by Plains Indians scared Texas settlers. Apaches terrorized settlers in North Texas. Comanches and Kiowas raided farms and ranches all over the Texas territory. By the mid-1800s, most Texans feared and hated Native Americans of any kind.

What was left of the Caddo confederacies had been moved to a place on the Brazos River close to present-day Waco, Texas. The Caddo population had been reduced to less than 1,000. The United States government decided to round up all the settled Native Americans in east and north Texas and send them to a reservation. They were confined on the Brazos River reservation "for their own protection." There was, however, no protection on the reservation. Apaches continued to steal from them, and bands of settlers gathered to kill them.

In 1859, a mob of 250 settlers invaded the lower part of the Brazos River reservation. Only fifty Native American men were there to defend against the mob. A gun battle followed. All but one of the Native Americans made it back to the reservation. Then the mob of Texans threatened to attack the reservation and kill all the natives. Major Robert Neighbors, the newly appointed federal agent to the Texas Indians who was in charge of their safety,

The seal of the Caddo Nation, pictured here, is an emblem of the Caddos' traditions.

requested help from both the Texas and the U.S. governments. The Texas governor did nothing. The U.S. government sent two lieutenants and eighty soldiers to the area. The only thing to be done was keep the Native Americans confined to the reservation. That put Major Neighbors and the Native Americans in a difficult situation. The Texas summer promised to be severely hot, and water was scarce. Already weakened from the lack of provisions, many Native Americans were sick and some died. Water on the reservation was quickly evaporating, and what was left had become polluted and unfit to drink. If they left the reservation, though, the Native Americans would be killed.

Major Neighbors wanted to take the Native Americans to safety across the Red River into the Indian Territory in Oklahoma. His requests were ignored. When the face-off over water at the Brazos River reservation became dangerous, Neighbors got permission to move the Native Americans to Oklahoma.

The trail across the Red River was as dangerous as the unstable conditions at the Brazos River reservation. Apaches attacked. Water was scarce. Temperatures held at over 100 degrees every day. Two days into the trip, the soldiers assigned to protect the Native Americans were recalled. Major Neighbors and a few soldiers under his command stayed with the Native Americans until they reached the Washita River where they were to stay. On September 1, 1859, the major took a census of those in his care. Only 244 Caddo had made it to Oklahoma. Major Neighbors was subsequently murdered in Texas for helping the Caddo. He was shot by a group of white settlers just after his return.

The Caddo settled on the Washita River reservation. The Jerome Act of 1892, however, did away with the reservation. Each Caddo person was given a piece of land. The rest of the reservation land was opened for public sale.

The Brazos River, shown here in the present day, was the site of many confrontations for the Caddo.

The Oklahoma Indian Welfare Act of 1938 required the Caddo to change their traditional tribal government. The system of *caddi* and *connas* ended. In 1938, the Caddo adopted a corporate charter and gained recognition for self-government. By the 1970s, the Caddo decided the corporate organization was not working for them. A committee spent a year creating a workable constitution for tribal organization. This constitution was ratified in 1976.

Today, many Caddos still live around Anadarko and Binger, Oklahoma. Ancestors of modern Caddos had settled in these areas after being forced to leave their homes in Texas. Some Caddo have moved away. More than 3,500 names are on the tribal roll. Many Caddos work as artists, business people, government employees, and degreed professionals. Tribal leadership is no longer in the hands of men only. In 2000, Larue Parker was named chair of the Caddo tribe.

Though the Caddo have adopted the modern American lifestyle, they continue to teach their children the traditions of the tribe. Many festivals take place during the year. These include a number of social dances, where the Caddo continue to keep not only their dances, but also their tribal songs alive. They have recorded an album on Canyon Records entitled "Songs of the Caddo" and were recently inducted into the Oklahoma Music Hall of Fame for their contributions to keeping Native American music and tribal traditions alive.

The Caddo have many traditional dances, such as the Duck Dance, the Bell Dance, the Alligator Dance, and the Turkey Dance. The Alligator Dance, and the songs that go with it, speak of a time when the Caddo lived in Louisiana and Texas. The Turkey Dance, created by the Caddo, is one of the oldest of any Native American dances. It has a special sacredness to the Caddo as a remembrance of where they came from and the trials, journeys, and battles of their ancestors. The Caddo people have survived the obstacles of their past and are keeping their culture and traditions alive.

Timeline

5500 B.C.	Groups related to the Caddo live in the areas of present-day northwest Louisiana and northeast Texas, in the Red River area.
500 B.C.	Caddo learn to grow corn and other food crops.
1541	Hernando de Soto, a Spanish explorer, encounters the Caddo.
1684	René-Robert Cavalier, Sieur de La Salle, a French explorer, meets the Caddo.
1687	La Salle returns to Caddo territory to make allies of the Caddo confederacies. Spanish also court the Caddo as allies.
1762	France turns Louisiana Territory over to the Spanish. Caddos are no longer needed as allies by either France or Spain.
1800	Spain returns Louisiana Territory to France.
1803	France sells Louisiana Territory to the United States. Caddos are again living between two rivals—the United States east of the Red River and the Spanish territories west of the Red River.

1821	Mexico declares independence from Spain. Caddo chief (*caddi*) Dehahuit becomes a representative between the Native American nations, the Republic of Mexico, and the United States. Dehahuit works to resolve disputed boundaries between Mexico and the United States. Dehahuit dies in 1833 before resolving the boundary dispute.
1845	Texas joins the United States as the twenty-eighth state in the union.
1850s	Caddo and other Texas Native Americans are moved to a reservation close to the Brazos River. In 1859, Caddos are removed from Texas to Oklahoma.
1892	The Jerome Act eliminates the reservation system.
1936–1938	Oklahoma Indian Welfare Act requires the Caddo to change their traditional tribal government. Caddos adopt a corporate charter for their tribal government.
1976	Caddo reorganize and write a constitution for tribal government. Constitution ratified.
2000	Larue Parker becomes chairperson of the Caddo in Oklahoma.

Glossary

Ah-ah Ha'-yo (AH-ah HA-yo) Great Father Above; refers to the Caddo supreme being. The spelling reflects current Caddo usage.

alliance (uh-LY-uhns) A friendly agreement to work together.

ancestry (AN-sehs-tree) Members of a family who lived before those members who are alive now.

anthropologists (an-thruh-PAH-luh-gihsts) Scholars who study the life, ways, and beliefs of different people around the world.

amayxoya (ah-may-sho-uh) War hero.

caddi (kad-dee) Chief of a Caddo tribe. Literally, "true chief" or "real chief."

canahas (kuna-has) A subordinate headman or village elder.

communal (kuh-MYOO-nehl) Shared by several people, as in a communal shelter.

confederacy (kuhn-FEHD-uh-ruh-see) A union of tribes with a common purpose.

connas (KOHN-nas) Priests who helped the *xinesi* with religious rites. They were also medicine men.

guild (GIHLD) A group or organization of people who do the same kind of work or who have the same interests.

jerky (JUR-kee)   Dried strips of meat.

presidios (prih-SEE-dee-ohz)   Military posts under Spanish control.

staple (STAY-puhl)   Any food or product that is used regularly and kept in large amounts.

tammas (tuhm-mas)   Caddo tribal messengers and police.

thatch (THACH)   Roof or wall covering made from straw, grass, or reeds.

xinesi (TSA-neh-see)   Literally, "Mr. Moon." Religious leader of the Caddo.

Resources

BOOKS

Archer, Jane. *Texas Indian Myths and Legends*. Plano, TX: Republic of Texas Press, 2000.

Carter, Cecile Elkins. *Caddo Indians: Where We Came From*. Norman, OK: University of Oklahoma Press, 2001.

Cassidy Jr., James J. *Reader's Digest Through Indian Eyes: The Untold Story of Native American Peoples*. Pleasantville, NY: The Reader's Digest Association, 1995.

Edmondson, J.R. *The Alamo Story, From Early History to Current Conflict*. Plano, TX: Republic of Texas Press, 2000.

Glover, William B. "A History of the Caddo Indians." *Louisiana Historical Quarterly*, Vol. 18, No. 4, October 1935.

LeVere, David. *The Caddo Chiefdoms*. Lincoln, NE: University of Nebraska Press, 1998.

Newcomb Jr., W.W. *The Indians of Texas, From Prehistoric to Modern Times*. Austin, TX: University of Texas Press, 1961.

Perttula, Timothy K. *The Caddo Nation*. Austin, TX: University of Texas Press, 1992.

Simon, Nancy, and Evelyn Wolfson. *American Indian Habitats*. New York: David McKay Company, 1977.

Smith, F. Todd. *The Caddo, the Wichitas, and the United States, 1846-1901*. College Station, TX: Texas A&M Press, 1996.

——. *The Caddo Indians, Tribes at the Convergence of Empires, 1542-1854*. College Station, TX: Texas A&M Press, 1995.

ORGANIZATIONS

Caddo Nation of Oklahoma
Cultural Preservation Department
P.O. Box 487
Binger, OK 73009
(405) 656-2901

Indian Territory Museum and Library
P.O. Box 65
Caddo, OK 74729
(580) 367-2787

WEB SITES

Due to the changing nature of Internet links, PowerKids Press has developed an online list of Web sites related to the subject of this book. This site is updated regularly. Please use this link to access the list:

www.powerkidslinks.com/lna/caddo

Index